The **Balder**
The **Better**

Telly Savalas (left) and friend. "Baldness takes us back to Day One and the way we looked when we first came into this world," Savalas once said. "'Bald is beautiful' was the first comment we made."

The Balder
The Better

Peter Taylor

KEY PORTER BOOKS

Canadian Cataloguing in Publication Data

Taylor, Peter
The balder the better

ISBN 1-55013-874-X

1. Baldness. I Title.

PN6231.B27T393   1997   391.5   C97-931297-3

The publisher gratefully acknowledges the support of the Canada Council for the Arts and the Ontario Arts Council for its publishing program.

THE CANADA COUNCIL | LE CONSEIL DES ARTS
FOR THE ARTS | DU CANADA
SINCE 1957 | DEPUIS 1957

Key Porter Books Limited
70 The Esplanade
Toronto, Ontario
Canada M5E 1R2

Design: Leah Gryfe
Electronic formatting: Heidi Palfrey

Printed and bound in Canada

97 98 99 00 6 5 4 3 2 1

Boom, We're Bald

Current demographers seem more than a little obsessed by the fact that over the next very few years, some fifty gazillion young men around the world will have just turned, or will be about to turn, fifty. This book, then, is for them. If, as has been often said, every hair lost is a lesson learned, then the world is in very fine hands indeed.

"I used to wear a rug, and then I decided that bald says integrity—right?"

Contents

•

●

Patrick Stewart, still baldly going where no one has gone before . . .

Hair-Raising Tales

A S A MEMBER OF THE BALDING (AND FINALLY BALD) fraternity for more than thirty years, I am convinced that hair is responsible for more than badly clogged drains.

On the shoulder or lapel of a man's suit, for instance, one lone, long hair of the wrong color has been known to trigger frightfully unfortunate misunderstandings.

On expensive carpeting, even the smallest, damp hairball is enough to put you off your food for the rest of the day.

In finer restaurants, a single hair in a bowl of soup is one too many, I say.

Hair of the dog, on the other hand, is fine, as far as I'm concerned.

ALAIN JUPPÉ • DOONESBURY'S DUKE • JOHN T. CAPPS III • SEAN CONNERY

INTRODUCTION

·····

The B Files

AN ANCIENT MANUSCRIPT: A PROPHECY

"If you thought the Sixties and its Age of Aquarius were cause for celebration," she said, handing me the dusty manuscript, "then you are probably old and wise enough today to be told that it was little more than a way-stop, a warm-up, a raggedy-assed rehearsal for the momentous significance of the new millennium."

I hadn't seen Charlene in six years, and I was immediately struck by the fact that her once bouncing, blonde mane of big hair had been reduced to a buzz-cut.

"You and your ancient manuscripts," I laughed, staring into

ALAIN JUPPÉ · DOONESBURY'S DUKE · JOHN T. CAPPS III · SEAN CONNERY her huge blue eyes. "What ever happened to that fellow Greenfield and his Celestial Prophecies?"

"His name was Redfield, and it was Celestine," she corrected me twice. "Trust me on this one, Jocko. A dozen insights wouldn't add up to what's in here."

I listened. You have to respect a woman who gives up a perfectly good newspaper job to go traveling around the world doing research on cultural and demographic changes for the U.N. We ordered our second bottle of wine—a robust Rhône—and filled our glasses.

"According to this document," she began, "the year 2000 will be especially important . . . extremely important to people like you . . ."

"Will it be the end of the world, as many have always said it will?" I interrupted her. "I won't have to pay my American Express?"

"Bigger than that," she replied, flashing her famous smile and wiping the dust from her very large hands on the linen tablecloth.

"God's coming back to see how we're doing, he's going to be on 'Jeopardy'?" I grinned.

"Not even warm, and please be serious."

ALBERT EINSTEIN • SENATOR JAKE GARN • KEN KESEY • SHAQUILLE O'NEIL

I checked my tendency to joke about things I don't have time to understand. "Will computers fail? And will that matter?"

"Yes, and no." She smiled enigmatically.

"Will the Leafs win the Stanley Cup? Will Buffalo finally win the Super Bowl?" I blurted.

She smiled that famous smile again. "Look at that date," she said, lifting away the parchment cover from the package in my lap.

And there, in what was clearly that back-slanted, awkward scrawl of left-handed people doing their very best, was written:

> *Copyright © 1000*
> *All Rights Reserved*
> *No part of this Manuscript may be rewritten or*
> *"reproduced" by any means now known or hereafter*
> *invented without permission of*

The signature scrawled beneath that curious copyright was unintelligible, but for the first letter of the writer's name, which was unmistakably a "B," and farther along, upon closer scrutiny, the letter "i," which, while it couldn't have been, appeared to be dotted—I swear—with a little "happy face."

ALBERT EINSTEIN · SENATOR JAKE GARN · KEN KESEY · SHAQUILLE O'NEIL

"Wow, this was written in the year 1000!" I exclaimed, drawing curious glances from other diners in the room.

"Hush!" Charlene admonished. "There have already been several attempts to steal this stuff. God knows, I've been threatened, and I have also been offered huge sums of cash to suppress it. So please lower your voice."

Signaling the waiter for another bottle of wine—a 1995 Beaujolais—Charlene continued.

"For an entire century, according to the Manuscript, the year 1000 was awaited with special anticipation. The three perfect circles in 1000 became a symbol of hope for people throughout the world, or at least the world as people knew it at the time. The year 1000, according to the seers and prophets, would be the year of the final freedom."

"The final freedom?"

"Yes," she said, sliding a scarlet fingernail across the brittle page, "though you'll notice here that they spelled it 'freedome.'"

"Aha," I said, genuinely intrigued.

"Dome. As in head. Get it? Dome as in those three perfect circles. Free. Dome." Charlene stared at me over the top of her glasses.

"Heads free of hair!" I almost shouted.

"You got it, Pontiac. According to prophecy—lots and lots of it, I might add—the year 1000 would mark the zenith of the evolution of mankind. The final 'freedome' would have arrived, and the transformation of man from the hairy beast of the jungle to 'smooth guy' would finally be complete."

"Smooth guy?" I said, wrinkling my brow in puzzlement.

"Jacob, in Genesis," she said. "The one who said, 'Behold, Esau my brother is a hairy man, and I am a smooth man.'"

"Wow."

According to Charlene, most people wanted evolution to be finished. They'd had it with evolution. They'd leaned to walk, and talk, and pick up girls, and they just wanted to get on with their lives. The way they saw it, becoming the "smooth man" alluded to in Genesis would be their final break with the animal kingdom. "Freedome At Last" became a kind of battle cry. And yet, despite all of this, in the years leading up to 1000, there were many other people for whom hair had suddenly become one hell of an obsession.

"It was as if some powerful, genetic tie to the animal world was fighting for its life," Charlene said. "As if the hairy beast in all of us was refusing to go along with God's—or Mother Nature's—master plan, or go away."

I refilled our glasses.

"Suddenly, you got hair everywhere," Charlene said. "People growing it down to here."

I leaned to look under the table where Charlene was pointing. In the six years since I had seen her, I had almost forgotten how very long her legs were... how long, and lovely.

"People were spending hours combing their hair, fluffing it, teasing it, washing it, brushing, braiding, and coloring it with vegetable dyes. They were plaiting it, weaving it into cornrows, and fashioning it into what we now call ponytails. According to the Manuscript, in the year 967 I think it was, people began performing plays about hair, including what we now call musicals. It got so bad for a while that no one was getting any work done. Seriously, it was a terrible time."

"Wow," was all I could say.

"'Wow'? My God, here we are talking about a crucial moment in the history of mankind, a moment the prophets had predicted would mark the final separation of man and ape, and you say 'Wow.' Why, I can remember a time when you cared about things like this."

"So what happened?" I asked, drumming my fingers on the tabletop.

"Nothing," she said, and for a moment there, I thought she was about to cry.

"Nothing?"

"Well, nothing good, nothing of lasting value. In fact, the ancient equivalent of marketing men, and women, got into the act, and suddenly those three perfect circles were everywhere. They appeared on the stonework around temples and libraries. They showed up in paintings. The T-shirt hadn't been invented yet, but ancient entrepreneurs got into the act, made goofy cartoon stencils, and were hawking T-Togas, and T-Tunics, and T-Robes in the streets. Men kept fussing with the hair they had, and worrying about the ones that went floating down the aqueduct. Overnight, a wig and hat trade was flourishing where once there had been hope. Baldness, instead of being seen as a sign of the final break with our animal past, made people nervous, and everywhere you looked men had taken to wearing silly hats and helmets, and gluing tufts of animal fur to the tops of their heads."

"So the year 1000, with its three symbolic circles, came and went," I said softly, "and man learned nothing?"

Charlene had been staring at me intently as she recounted the buildup and letdown on either side of the year 1000. Suddenly, almost conspiratorially, she looked over her left shoulder, then her right, then back at me. "Until now," she whispered.

Charlene has always had a thing for bald men. Make a list of her weaknesses, and bald writers would be right up there near the top. I felt her knee press against mine under the table.

"The year 2000, the new millennium, don't you see? It's all in the Manuscript. According to 'B,' the prophets were right. The bones, the entrails, the stars—whatever—they were basically right about everything. The three circles and the final 'freedome' fit hand in hand, just like they said."

"So what went wrong?"

"Unfortunately," Charlene sighed, "they made a mistake."

"Mistake?"

"Yeah, they forgot to carry the one or something."

"Carry the one?"

"Well, that part is difficult to read, but as nearly as I can make it out, 'B' sat down at the end of the year—on New Year's Eve, I think it was—and put the whole damned thing through the hopper one more time."

"And?"

"And, it turns out, 'freedome' will arrive in the year 2000."

"The prophets were out by 1,000 years?"

"According to the Manuscript."

Ordering another bottle of wine, I struggled with the enormity of Charlene's discovery. And as the waiter proffered his recommendation—a Merlot from a small but highly regarded winery at Sète in the south of France—I wondered why, of all the men in her life, she had chosen me as the one with whom to share the secrets of this ancient folio. As if reading my mind, Charlene carefully poured a dribble of the Vin de Pays d'Oc into her saucer. Then, dipping the base of her wine glass into the redness of the spill three times, she proceeded to stamp three perfect circles onto the white linen of the tablecloth.

"You in? Or out?" she said.

I stared at the three perfect circles on the tabletop. It might have been the wine, or the bottle of Grand Marnier we had shared with our dessert, but suddenly I found myself agreeing with everything Charlene (or "B") said. And as I followed her beautiful fingertip along each spidery line of the elegant calligraphy, it all made perfect sense.

Baldness, as symbolized by the three perfect circles in Charlene's Manuscript, was the shining proof.

Baldness, as depicted by the round, red stains on the tablecloth, stood for freedom from the past.

"Freedome" from the charlatans and hucksters with their snake-oil cures and their yak-fur rugs.

"Freedome" from vanity, and medicine cabinets stuffed to overflowing with hair-care products.

"Freedome" from the hair of our hairy ancestors.

I was in.

Sensing the moment of my conversion, Charlene immediately set about explaining the urgency of the mission. "There's very little time," she said. "You must start today. According to 'B,' unless someone steps forward to carry the banner, there is a very grave danger that the year 2000 will come and go with little to mark its passing but trinkets, and trash, and shoddy souvenirs.

"The Manuscript says that whoever is chosen must be fearless, for he will again be up against false prophets and hucksters by the score. There will be publishers with coffee-table books, and even paperbacks purporting to contain the essential knowledge of the past 1,000 years. According to the Manuscript, there will be coffee mugs, key chains, beer steins, and a commemorative reissue of Kubrick's *2001*.

"Most of all, the Manuscript warns against anti-evolutionary forces, the ancestral tug of our animal selves—the call of the wild, I suppose you might say—and those who would align themselves with it."

Charlene went on to say that the author of the Manuscript warned specifically against the scourge of the wig-seller, and others who would certainly strive to invent new ways of keeping baldness from shining through. According to the Manuscript, the person chosen to spread the word would have to compile lists of great bald men through the centuries, and their "likenesses," which Charlene and I interpreted to mean photographs. He would have to collect citations and quotations extolling the strengths and virtues of bald and balding men.

In a curiously modern usage of the word, the author of the Manuscript wrote: "The year 2000 must be a time for 'outing' all who would seek to hide or otherwise disguise their superiority over the beasts of the fields, the forests, the jungles hereabouts. For failing that, these prophecies shall amount to naught, and mankind shall remain in concert with the hairy beasts of the animal world for yet another one thousand years."

According to Charlene, it was the description of the person chosen to carry the torch that had reminded her of me. According to old "B," whoever it was would need to be not only fearless, but tall, bald, and handsome; worldly, sophisticated, virile, and athletic.

"And look right here," she said pointing to the page from which she had been reading. "It says the chosen one, above everything else, must have a good sense of humor."

I smiled.

I had hoped that Charlene would agree to a layover, but she was off to Paris to meet a dealer who had unearthed what he claimed were the missing notebooks of Nostradamus. She hoped to be back on this continent a week later, she said, to look at photographs of strange graffiti that Neil Armstrong claimed to have brought back from the moon. And then off to Mexico to see Carlos Castaneda, and then . . .

"God has made very few perfect heads. The rest of them he covered with hair."

—U.S. Senator Jake Garn

"Behold, Esau my brother is a hairy man, and I am a smooth man."

—Jacob, Genesis 27:11

CHAPTER ONE

·····

Baldness 2000

If the three perfect circles in the year 2000 represent three bald heads, this could be the best news you've ever had!

If you're thinning or receding, you're well on the way.

If you're totally bald, you're already there.

If you fall into neither category, watcha gonna do?

Will you join your bald, bold, beautiful brothers in celebrating this pinnacle of the evolution of man?

Or are you going to remain with your long-armed, knuckle-dragging cousins from the enchanted forest?

What's it going to be?

STIRLING MOSS · ARTURO TOSCANINI · FRANK SINATRA · TELLY SAVALAS

"Take it all off."

To be or not to be . . .

What was the question?

"Freedom's just another word
for nothin' left to lose."

—Kris Kristofferson

CHAPTER TWO

· · · · ·

Hair Today

Theories come, and theories go, much to the delight of theorists, I suppose. Each age in turn—with the science available to it at the time—attempts to shed some light upon the great unanswered questions of the day.

Where does the wind go when it doesn't blow?

Who put the overalls in Mrs. Murphy's chowder?

How you gonna keep 'em down on the farm after they've seen "Paree"?

Why do I love you like I do, do, do?

How many roads must a man walk down?

What do women really want?

BALDWIN THE BALD · SUSAN POWTER · TERRY BRADSHAW · BING CROSBY

What kind of fool am I?

The question "What causes baldness?" has been on that list since time began.

Everybody and his shaggy dog seems to have a theory of his own. One very good friend of mine with a thick mane of gray hair suggests the following. According to him, as your hair grows, the roots plunge downward into and through your scalp. When they hit gray matter, they turn gray. When they hit nothing, according to this old coot, they fall out.

Socrates, until the courts awarded him a glass of hemlock in 399 B.C., went about Athens telling anyone who would listen that baldness was caused by too much sex. "Hey you," he was fond of yelling at every bald or balding Greek he encountered in the city's many coffee shops and shish-kebab restaurants. "Find another hobby! Get a life!"

Aristotle, himself bald at a very early age, was of the opinion that baldness was the end result of too much brain activity in the frontal lobes. (Take a look at Einstein's forehead. See if you don't agree.)

And so it goes, even unto the present day.

Recent studies at North Carolina State University have a theory

Albert Einstein: Did the fact that both parents were bald lead him to his theory of relativity?

about the female hormone estrogen to add to the incredible series of postulations put forward to explain why some men "got it" and some men "don't."

According to *The Proceedings of the National Academy of Sciences*, Dr. Robert Smart (who you'd think would know better) and graduate assistant Hye-Sun Oh were applying pesticides to mice. They wanted to see whether or not the pesticides bothered the mice's skin cancer. But what they found was that the shaved skin of mice grew hair when treated with an estrogen blocker.

Ergo (or, as they say in science, "Hey, come-and-take-a-look-at-this!"), if hair can be caused to grow by blocking estrogen, then maybe that "ole debil" estrogen caused hair not to grow in the first place. (Or something like that.)

North Carolina, curiously, is also the home of John T. Capps III. Capps, of Morehead City—not too far down the road from the university—is the founder and president of BHMA (Bald Headed Men of America).

Coincidence, or what?

ON THE OTHER SIDE OF THE SCIENTIFIC FENCE, EQUALLY credible researchers state just as firmly that an overabundance of estrogen is what gives so many men such pretty hair. And that estrogen shots, therefore, should reduce hair loss in men.

But before you rush off to the mall for a jug of that joy juice, consider the following:

1. A sudden infusion of female hormones into a healthy male body will likely waltz you from the bass to the soprano section of your choir quicker than you can say "Shave and a haircut..."

2. While an estrogen diet will undoubtedly give you a beautiful complexion, I'm told that if you guzzle enough of the stuff, you will probably grow breasts.

3. And finally, I'm sure I read this somewhere: just a spoonful of estrogen is capable of reducing your pecker to the size of a peanut in about the time it takes to go to the fridge for a beer.

If body chemistry—and not evolution—is a cause of baldness, however, it's the male hormone, testosterone, that gets my vote.

This is the one the scientists call super-juice—hormones that play Australian Rules.

●

THE DALAI LAMA · GEOFFREY HOLDER · WILLIAM MASTERS · MEL BLANC

Dear Mr. Bald Guy:

Is it true that bald-headed men care more about their partners during lovemaking than they do about themselves?

Doubtful and Curious in Baltimore

Dear Doubtful and Curious:

It is true that the energy some people spend on the business of growing and maintaining hair can make them weary and therefore thoughtless in matters of love. You two ladies should find your-self a bald lover and check it out. My guess is you'll agree.

Mr. Bald Guy

Testosterone is the hormone that gives your voice its edge of authority. And it probably goes a long way toward explaining why you prefer martinis, Scotch whisky, or beer to sangria and pousse-café.

In the fetus, testosterone is responsible for the development of male genitalia, and later, at puberty, it accounts for the continued growth of that same equipment.

In short, it determines the cut of your jib—it's the thing that makes a man of you.

And it is precisely a man's maleness, according to leading dermatologists around the world, that helps to make him bald.

Too much sex, too much thinking, estrogen, testosterone, or the progress of evolution.

Take your pick.

But while you're pondering, rest assured that ten things that do not cause or contribute to baldness are:

- Watching "Monday Night Football"
- Taping the Super Bowl
- Martinis
- Beer
- Cigars

MARK MESSIER · THOMAS KENEALLY · BRUCE WEBER · GEORGE FOREMAN

- Political incorrectness
- Masturbation
- Red meat
- A high IQ
- Refusing to use a map when lost

Ten things, on the other hand, that studies point to as possible contributors to baldness in men are as follows:

- ✶ An inquiring mind
- ✶ A lively wit and unstoppable sense of humor
- ✶ A fanatical desire to have women experience orgasm before you do
- ✶ Extraordinary success at love and business
- ✶ An odd charisma
- ✶ Money
- ✶ The ability to solve problems easily
- ✶ A magnetic personality
- ✶ Heredity (beautiful parents are much, much more than the luck of the draw)
- ✶ A large penis for your age, weight, and height

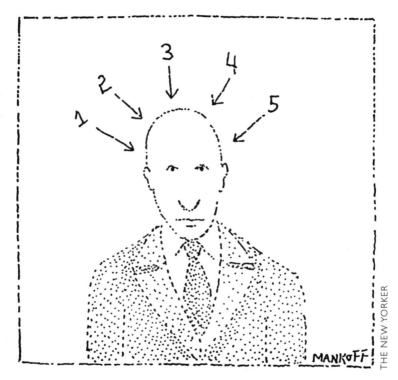

The Five Major Warning Signs of Baldness

"A man of my resources
cannot presume to have
a hairstyle...
get on and cut it."

—Winston Churchill

CHAPTER THREE

·····

B Is for Baldness

"Bald Is Beautiful," someone wrote a few years back, which may explain why, as we approach the year 2000, more and more men today are shaving their heads instead of sitting around waiting for it to happen.

But whether you've shaved your head or come by your baldness naturally, one thing is certain—you're part of a very exclusive club.

IN THE 1940S AND '50S WE HAD IKE, WINSTON CHURCHILL, and Charles de Gaulle.

In the 1960s we had Yul Brynner in *The King and I.*

MOSHE DAYAN · TUTANKHAMEN · CHARLES BARKLEY · HENRY MILLER

Yul Brynner

Pablo Picasso

On the stage, at the easel, or at the helms
of nations, the bald and balding stand
like beacons throughout our history,
touchstones against which lesser, hairier
men should measure themselves.

Winston Churchill

The 1970s gave us the macho swagger of Telly Savalas as TV's chrome-domed detective, Kojak.

In the 1980s, especially after doffing his hairpiece in *Never Say Never Again*, women who had always found him attractive began to talk about an even sexier Sean Connery.

In the 1990s, as the super-cool Captain Jean-Luc Picard of "Star Trek, The Next Generation," Patrick Stewart took control as the sexy bald man women think about when they think about such things.

Since time began, it seems each decade has produced a poster guy, and as we approach the new millennium, the list of bald and balding heroes grows.

Daniel Benzali shaved his locks, hitting paydirt and stardom as the hairless, high-priced attorney Ted Hoffman in TV's "Murder One."

Michael Jordan and Danny DeVito give a whole new meaning to "walking tall."

When "The Three Tenors" hit the stage and the lights come up, it's the rapidly thinning (on top at least) Luciano Pavarotti who steals the show.

At Wimbledon and other venues around the world, the tennis groupies swoon for André Agassi.

BUDDHA · TOM PAXTON · HUNTER S. THOMPSON · PERSIS KHAMBATTA

Rob Reiner

Jeremy Rifkin

Phil Collins

Mustaches, beards, and musical skill can't begin to hide or disguise true genius—the BS™ (Bald Spot) says it all.

Dr. Hunter S. Thompson spreads fear and loathing across the literary landscape, tilting at windbags while kicking ass.

Not only does he just look better, but I happen to think that Bruce Willis's acting has actually improved since he began shaving his head.

Aren't the Fordham Baldies your very favorite teenage gang in Ken Wahl's cult classic *The Wanderers*?

Yes, baldness is the '90s, and beyond.

It is the final attitude, the cool frontier, the cocky look of those in-your-face high-fashion shoots, television drama, the new action movies, and life on the edge.

It is the shaved-head, tough-guy trademark of those awesome athletes on the football field, the basketball court, or in the ring.

Baldness smacks of toughness, sleekness, importance, power, authority, self-confidence, honesty, and self-control.

And for all of those reasons—and then some—it makes hairy men very nervous, and strong women weak in the knees.

So, Why all the Fuzz?

What is it about bald-headed men?

Why, throughout history, have so many of them risen head and shoulders above their contemporaries?

HAILE SELASSIE · NAPOLEON · HENRY ADAMS · VLADIMIR I. LENIN

Calvin Trillin

DJ Cliff Dumas

Baldness, a friend writes, is a lot like talent, money, sex, or 1950s rock and roll—you can never have too much of it.

Bob Hoskins

Danny DeVito, walking tall.

Oh, what a time it was! As anyone over the age of fifty will tell you, it was the Eisenhower presidency—not the Kennedy, and not (God forbid) the Nixon—that defined an era, giving us Happy Days, ducktails, blue suede shoes, and old time rock and roll by the jukeboxful. "I like Ike" was the slogan of the day, and although we might not have known it back then, the man himself was a role model we'd come to admire.

Is it just a strong-man, father-figure fixation, or is there some deeper, darker reason why women are drawn to bald-headed men like bees to honey, like moths to a flame?

Like the peacock's tail, or the pronged and horny rack of a rutting elk, baldness is, in fact, a sexual traffic light, switched on by Mother Nature to identify the virile male.

For women, it signals green for GO—for other men, it flashes RED.

Why then, despite the wealth of evidence suggesting that the bald and balding among us have always been (and continue to be) our leading lights, are there so many bad disguises, so many men doing such dumb things to cover up that traffic light?

If you didn't like your face, would you wear a mask?

Go figure.

"It is ironic that a man should consider his bald head a sign of lost virility, because it is precisely a male's maleness that helps make him bald."

—Sylvia Rosenthal
Cosmetic Surgery: A Consumer's Guide

CHAPTER FOUR

· · · · ·

Generation B

If predictions are true, and those three perfect circles in the year 2000 do mark the ultimate rung on the ladder of evolution, what better way to celebrate this grand millennium than a three-pronged attack on the hairy enemies of baldness everywhere?

We must start immediately to develop an "old boys'" network of bald-pride spokesmen. We need bold, bald role models—be they entertainers, sportsmen, or politicians—from around the world.

We must attack the seedy, greedy world of commerce where it hurts, exposing the hypocrisy of transplants, wigs and weaves, and other cover-ups.

And we must begin today, with a systematic but gentle

CHARLES DE GAULLE · HOMER SIMPSON · PABLO PICASSO · YUL BRYNNER

"Then one day we decided 'To hell with hair!'"

"outing" of those thousands among us who have been brow-beaten into hiding their baldness under all manner of silly disguise.

FROM THE FOLKS WHO PUT THE SHAM IN THE POO ...

Hair-care products line miles of shelf space in drugstores and supermarkets. Television commercials and half-hour infomercials bombard us with news of "cures," restoratives, and cover-ups of every description.

J. Crew and Victoria's Secret catalogues arrive every three weeks with nary a bald head in those otherwise glossy pages.

Prison and sports movies aside, the television and movie industries seem tied to a star system that would deny leading roles to all but a few of our leading lights.

The President of the United States gets a haircut, and the media goes wild with jokes about Hair Force One.

Given the size of the forces aligned against us, it is no small wonder that many men, otherwise magnificently bald, choose to hide that baldness through all manner of silly subterfuge and dastardly disguise.

Enough's enough!

The time has come to call a halt to all of that.

In the words of the Bald Headed Men of America, "If you haven't got it, flaunt it!"

Or, as John Prine sings so wonderfully in "Dear Abby," "You are what you are, and you ain't what you ain't."

Well, you know who you are.

And if you don't, we do.

There are five main groups in what we choose to christen the Bald Hall of Shame. In the year 2000, let's "out" them!

WIND SOCKS & SIDEWINDERS

It is entirely possible, if you grow it long enough, to take the hair from one side of your head and comb it across the top of your skull to the other. But why? In Winnipeg or Chicago, a person adopting this particular pretense will have to spend the rest of his life walking counter-clockwise to the wind.

There are variations on this theme, of course.

While we doubt anyone ever managed the tired old joke about growing his eyebrows long enough to sweep back over his forehead, there is the well-known twist on the ponytail, in which certain of our bald brothers comb squid-like tentacles of hair from the back to the front of their heads.

Trust us. Calling it a "Caesar cut" just doesn't cut it. It was laughed at in Caesar's time (behind the Emperor's back, of course), and, after all these years, it still gets a laugh.

ROAD KILL

Like car crashes, we know we shouldn't look at them, but we have to, right?

You've seen them.

You can't miss them.

One Color—One Size—Fits All!

You can spot these shaggy, straw-like things nine blocks away. They're always colored reddish-brown and seem to shout "If you don't know I'm wearing a wig, you probably need glasses!"

We were not totally surprised to learn that these things are made mostly in Taiwan (from yak fur, for God's sake) by the very same people who produce—you guessed it—those nose, mustache, and glasses disguises (think Groucho Marx) that are so popular at office Christmas parties and Hallowe'en.

Elton John

Sam Donaldson

101 Uses for a Dead Cat?

*T*HE *B*IGWIG

Here the rug merchants really clean up. This is road kill for the very rich. Like the finest Oriental carpets, they are sold by the square inch. ABC TV's Sam Donaldson, Frank Sinatra, Paul Simon, and British rocker Gary Glitter come to mind. Burt Reynolds (before he got real) wore one. TV's Larry Hagman. William Shatner of "Star Trek." "Why?" you ask. Why indeed? Imagine spending thousands of dollars to hear your friends and neighbors say, "Hey, nice wig."

Are these the people Leonard Cohen is talking about when he sings his ballad "Everybody Knows"?

*D*R. *S*EUSS *L*IVES*!* *T*HE *M*AD *H*ATTERS

These are the cats you never see without hats. Cowboy hats, bowlers, beanies, toques, baseball hats, Tilleys, turbans, and tams—you name it, someone's wearing it to cover up.

Santa Claus, Stompin' Tom Connors, Roy Rogers, Yasser Arafat, the Pope, and probably the entire College of Cardinals are guilty on this front.

Mad hatters all!

Yasser Arafat

Stompin' Tom Connors

Pope John Paul II

Like Roy Rogers, the Lone Ranger, Santa Claus, and Jimmy Durante, Stompin' Tom, Yasser, and John Paul II seem hell bent—and then some—on hiding the fact that they are no hairier than thou.

And Finally ... Chia Pets

Like the obscenely expensive wig, these one-man reforestation projects come close to matching the cost of a car. Like tiny potted plants, the little clumps and tufts are farmed into your head in rows by Mercedes-driving maniacs, intent on covering up the second most masculine feature on your entire body.

Our advice to you: spend that money on yourself. Buy a Mercedes convertible. Feel the wind on your head. Celebrate your baldness.

Join the fun.

"It so happens I like being bald!"

CHAPTER FIVE

·····

The B Spot

id you know that rubbing a bald spot is good luck? Did you know that if you are planning on having a baby, and rub a bald spot while wishing for a boy or girl, that wish can come true?

Did you know that spotting a bald spot on the street means your sex life is going to improve dramatically?

Did you know that dreaming about a bald spot means you are about to meet the man of your dreams?

Did you know that finding a bald head on your pillow in the morning means you've probably already met the guy?

CHRISTOPHER DARDEN · JACQUES CHIRAC · PHIL COLLINS · W.C. FIELDS

ƲIVE LA ℱRANCE

Plus ça change . . .

They gave us hunchbacks, haute cuisine, fine wines, and rude waiters. They gave us the Bastille, the Left Bank, the guillotine, the Eiffel Tower, and the Folies Bergere. Election after election, they place their trust in the hands of bald presidents and prime ministers with a sangfroid, a je ne sais quoi, and the ooh-la-la you would expect from a people who knit during revolutions.

Charles de Gaulle

François Mitterand

Jacques Chirac

Laurent Fabius

Alain Juppé

Dear Mr. Bald Guy:

I'm a 27-year-old heiress to an international brewing and distilling corporation. My friends tell me that I am stunningly beautiful, whatever that means. My previous boyfriends all admit that I'm better in bed than anyone they've ever known, but that I don't know when to stop, and end up tiring them out.

Lonely and Loaded in Boston

Dear Lonely and Loaded:

That was the sweetest, tenderest, most thoughtful and beautiful letter I have ever received in my life. Call me here at the office. NOT at home. I want to help you.

Mr. Bald Guy

Don't forget, NOT at home.

"We believe the hair replacement industry for men is like the cosmetic industry for women ... a giant black hole that will just suck your money away for the rest of your life."

—Christine Lavin
Life According to Four Bitchin' Babes (Volume Two)

CHAPTER SIX

Male Pattern Baldness and the Credibility Gap

As with any business that preys on vanity, the fact that the bald business has its own hairy-assed coterie of money-grubbing dorks should come as no surprise.

Let's face it, like those apes and chimpanzees who didn't make the evolution cut, there are some men for whom the rigors and demands of baldness are just as frightening as climbing down from that banana tree and walking tall.

Men who confuse hair with looks, indeed with their very selves.

"She doesn't like me, she likes my hair," they seem to be saying, suggesting—one supposes—that the lady in question is about to throw herself into the bathroom sink, or down the shower drain, in hot pursuit.

ROBERT MORLEY • COUNT BASIE • WILLIAM RANDOLPH HEARST • JOHN GLENN

Men who spend 15 to 20 minutes a day (that's 90 to 120 hours a year, for God's sake) fussing with that mass of dead hair cells atop their heads.

Men who—unlike Popeye—will never know the joy of standing bald and buck-naked in front of the mirror, thumping themselves on the chest and shouting, "I YAM WHAT I YAM!"

These are the guys who keep the medicine men happy and the rug merchants dancing in the market square.

You've seen the commercials—and infomercials—on late-night TV, the advertisements in daily newspapers and in magazines.

Does anyone honestly believe that stuff?

I'M NOT JUST THE PRESIDENT OF THE HAIR CLUB, I'M A MEMBER . . .

Those words, in case you've been on Pluto for the last few years, are from a ghastly television commercial that airs about 100 times between midnight and bedtime, 365 nights a year.

The speaker is the president of a firm that peddles cover-ups and, as if acknowledging the fact that most people might have just a little trouble trusting a guy with fake hair, he gives us a glimpse of his "before" picture.

ROBERT MORLEY · COUNT BASIE · WILLIAM RANDOLPH HEARST · JOHN GLENN

You see the photo for barely a nanosecond, but what you see is a pretty decent-looking guy. He looks like a neighbor who'd lend you stuff, a guy with opposable thumbs, who wouldn't upset you too much if he invited your sister to meet his folks.

He's not hiding anything. He looks honest, trustworthy, like maybe he knows who the hell he is.

But then the commercial flashes back to the president—the "member," as he likes to call himself—in his "after" incarnation, and right where the honesty used to shine through, you see this patch of brittle stuff that looks like cotton candy or fiberglass.

"Member" indeed!

ONE COLOR—ONE SIZE—FITS ALL!

Some people call them "road kill," while others refer to them as "artificial turf" or "cow patties," but someone out there is making hundreds of thousands of dollars peddling those dreadful thatches of reddish-brown stuff that looks like doll's hair and is about as attractive and obvious as a Tilley hat!

JUST PLUGGIN' AWAY

If someone walked up to you on the street and said, "I'm going to drill a whole bunch of little holes in your head, and then I'm going to rip little tufts of hair out of your arm pits, and out of your pubic patch, and maybe some from the back of your neck, and I'm gonna stuff that hair in those little holes in your head, and it's gonna grow!" you'd figure he was a street crazy, right?

Well, maybe they are *booga-booga*, but they are out there, and they are making money hand over fist. Did you know that the little personal reforestation projects carried out by these charlatans can set you back anywhere from $10,000 to $20,000? And that doesn't even include the watering or manure!

I Just Did My Hair and I'm Waiting For It to Dry

To quote syndicated columnist Dave Barry, "I'M NOT MAKING THIS UP!" There's a guy on American television who sells hair-colored paint. You read it right the first time—paint! (As in blond paint, auburn paint, brunette paint, and even gray paint.)

It comes in a spray can, and what you do is you shake it up, aim it at your baldness, and presto, you're on "The Dating Game"!

You laugh (I do every time I see him), but this guy has made so much money that instead of buying thirty-second or one-

DONOVAN BAILEY · PABLO CASALS · PETER GARRETT · DARRELL WALKER

minute spots, he buys advertisements that are as long as "Masterpiece Theatre."

How Ya Gonna Keep 'Em . . . ?

Of late, in print and on the World Wide Web, more and more references to "hair farming" are popping up. The mind does boggle as that image flashes by!

This procedure, according to the literature, doesn't involve fake hair, weaving, or painful surgery, but rather an expert manipulation of the scalp that will cause to sprout those thousands of hair roots lurking just under the surface of the scalp.

Yeah, right.

A Little Dab'll Do Ya . . .

And finally, of course, there's the altruistic pharmaceutical industry, ever in search of elixirs guaranteed to purge our minds and bodies of this week's woe.

Rogaine and Minoxidil appear to have gone the way of Martin and Lewis, thank goodness. But there will be others— newer, improved potions and lotions guaranteed to grow hair on everything from peaches to golf balls. For just as sure as God made little laboratory mice, some nutty professor is leaning over his cauldron right now with the toe of a frog and the eye of a newt.

Forget It, Guys

Be strong.

Be bold.

Flaunt your maleness.

Be bald!

An advisory panel of doctors reporting to the U.S. Food and Drug Administration states it loud and clear. Baldness in men is an inherited trait, and no product can make hair grow back on a bald head or keep the remaining strands from falling out. Nothing—absolutely nothing—done to the hair shaft once it emerges from the surface of the scalp will influence hair growth.

And that's that!

"Isn't it fantastic? They take these plugs from the back of your neck and put them on top of your head, and six months later it's a whole new ballgame."

"You are bald because you inherited an overload of testosterone. Use it."

—Guy Martin
Esquire

CHAPTER SEVEN

·····

Let's Face It

T alk to women the world over. Ask them this simple
question. Shipwrecked on a desert island, stuck in an
elevator, or maybe locked in a sleeping bag with a faulty
zipper, who'd you rather be with while waiting for help to arrive?

- Jack Nicholson, or Gene Shalit?
- Sir Anthony Hopkins, or Prince Charles?
- Mark Messier, or Charles Manson?
- André Agassi, or Michael J. Pollard?
- John Malkovich, or Jerry Lewis?
- Telly Savalas, or Nick the Greek?
- Michael Jordan, or Don King?
- Charles Barkley, or Little Richard?

DEMI MOORE · JASON ALEXANDER · BRIAN ENO · IDI AMIN · DADA

Jack Nicholson: ". . . hold the Brylcream, hold the hairspray, hold the mousse."

No matter where you travel, no matter how the question is put, the answers are likely to be the same.

Nicholson, Hopkins, Messier, Agassi, Malkovich, Savalas, Jordan, Barkley . . .

Let's face it. When it comes to sex appeal, desirability, or just plain old-fashioned lust, bald and balding men everywhere have a very ready, willing, and very biased fan club.

WHO'S SEXIER, MICHAEL JORDAN, OR DON KING?

That question was recently put to 407 extremely attractive women lined up for Patrick Stewart's autograph at a "Star Trek" convention in New York. Not surprisingly, 406 of them agreed that while waking up in Mr. King's bed might be a scary experience, climbing into Mr. Jordan's, they thought, might be a lot of fun.

The holdout, a Mrs. D. King from Brooklyn, N.Y., thought the boxing promoter was not only sexier but cuter, taller, a better basketball player, and made more money than the Chicago Bulls' celebrated, gazillionaire hoopster.

WHO'S SEXIER, SEAN CONNERY, OR HUGH GRANT?

For this assignment, our researchers traveled to Edinburgh,

Michael Jordan

Don King

Scotland, and that city's 307th Annual Haggis Bake-off and Sheep-Shearing Competitions. Here, the answers seemed to bear out our contention, time and time again—that when it comes to separating the men from the boys, there's no better guideline than a hairline, or, better still, the lack of one.

On the subject of Hugh Grant, the ladies were fair but firm in their resolve:

- "He'll nae be getting his wee caber tossed in these green hills, I'm tellin' you."
- "He wouldna ken a bonnie lassie from a Rin Tin Tin, that one, would he now?"
- "He'll nae be 'roamin' in my gloamin',' that's for sure."

Mention Sean Connery in these parts, however, and suddenly you're dealing with a plaid of a different color:

- "Aaah, there's a man for a' that … and then some."
- "Mr. Connery, Sean Connery? Now there's a fella can park his tired auld brogues under my auld bed any auld time."
- "Even as Dr. No, he made me want to say yes, yes, yes."

Who's sexier, we asked a group of ladies outside Madison Square Garden, Mark Messier, or Charlie Manson?

BURL IVES · DWIGHT D. EISENHOWER · JULIUS CAESAR · ZERO MOSTEL

Charles Barkley

Little Richard

Mark Messier

Charles Manson

Dear Mr. Bald Guy:

Through a remarkable combination of fantastic looks, a great sense of humor, and being pretty damn good in the "kitchen" (if you know what I mean, HA HA!), I've managed to snare myself three wonderful lovers. They all got lots of money, and they all buy me nice gifts whenever I hint that an expensive little something might cheer me up. Best of all, they all do what they're told. Unfortunately, I now have to make a choice, cuz I think the bozos are about to find out about each other. One of them is bald, one of them is losing his hair, and the other has really beautiful hair and is as cute as a button. Which one should I grab?

Running Out of Time in Toronto

Dear Running:

The one with the hair! The one with the hair!

Mr. Bald Guy

ALBERT EINSTEIN · U.S. SENATOR JAKE GARN · KEN KESEY · SHAQUILLE O'NEIL

The votes:

The New York Rangers, Number 11—99!

The Corcoran, California Solitaires, Number 6749216—0!

DRUNK:

"Shay, the top of your head feels just like my wife's breast."

GENTLEMAN:

"By God, so it does!"

ALBERT EINSTEIN • U.S. SENATOR JAKE GARN • KEN KESEY • SHAQUILLE O'NEIL

"Dear Sirs: Yes! I would like to learn more about Rogaine with minoxidil."

More Hair-Raising Tales

Hair, and what the folks still burdened with it call "hair care," can cost a body an arm and a leg these days.

In the 1970s, barbershops became "salons" overnight, barbers woke up as "stylists," and the price of a haircut soared from about $2.00 to the $25.00 level, where it sits today.

A brush and a comb and a bit of Wildroot Cream Oil don't get you far in a world that boasts more than 200 brands of shampoos, rinses, tints, conditioners, and sprays.

I see hair-dryers for guys selling at prices that make me dizzy. Hairy, no?

ALFRED HITCHCOCK · AMERICAN BALD EAGLE · E.T. · SINÉAD O'CONNOR

"You look like a walking phallus. You feel like it too."

—Geoffrey Holder
Actor, dancer, director of *The Wiz*

CHAPTER EIGHT

· · · · ·

The Super Dome

In Toronto they call it the SkyDome.

In New Orleans, it's the Superdome.

In Seattle, it's the Kingdome.

Calgary has its Saddledome, Houston, its Astrodome, and the Detroit Lions play in the Silverdome.

Considering the number of bald and razor-shorn skulls that kick, skate, punch, block, bat, run, punt, shoot, score, slam, and dunk their way into the record books, it should come as no surprise that more and more of our sports palaces and arenas have begun to name themselves in honor of these "domes."

Whatever the sport, wherever you travel, there they are.

ALLEN GINSBERG · ED ASNER · KING SOLOMON · GEORGES POMPIDOU

Toronto Raptors announcer Herbie Kuhn inducts a new recruit.

Throughout the history of professional sports, they are the stuff of legend.

The great "Bald Eagle" of the New York Giants, Y. A. Tittle.

Pittsburgh's Mel Blount and Terry Bradshaw.

The Oakland As' owner, Charlie O. Finlay, and Paul Hornung of the Green Bay Packers.

Remember Otis Sistrunk, the ex-Oakland Raider once referred to as an alumnus of the University of Mars by footballer-turned-broadcaster Alex Karras?

All superheroes.

All bald.

Today Mark Messier lights up Vancouver, even when the sun don't shine.

George Foreman has finally retired from the ring, but who'll soon forget that menacing skull?

Golfers Tom Weiskopf, Miller Barber, Tom Lehman, and Marc McCumber take baldness down the fairways, chasing big money on the close-cropped greens.

Michael Jordan, Shaquille O'Neal, and Charles Barkley aside, there are so many bald heads in the game of professional basketball today that for many U.S. fans, following the ball has become almost as tricky as following the puck in hockey games.

SIR ANTHONY HOPKINS · ED KOCH · LAURENT FABIUS · EDWARD VII

George Foreman

Darryl Strawberry and Evander Holyfield

Darrell Walker

Bruce Smith and Thurman Thomas
of the Buffalo Bills.

GENUS ENVY

Supermodel Eve Salvail

Grace Jones

Demi Moore

Sinéad O'Connor

"His heed was ballid,
that shone as eny glass."

—Chaucer

CHAPTER NINE

·····

The Bald Hall of Fame

Given the shining examples of bald leadership throughout history, and even the quickest look at the bald and balding luminaries of the present day, it is not surprising to learn that as many as a dozen cities throughout the world will soon be competing for the privilege of being home to the world's first Bald Hall of Fame.

London, Paris, New York, Toronto, Vancouver, and Tokyo are all expected to enter spirited bids.

Melbourne and Moscow should not be dismissed out of hand.

Rumor has it that Baltimore has considered changing its name to Baldimore in an effort to win favor with the ICBBM (International Council of Bald and Balding Men) in time for the selection.

ANDRÉ AGASSI · LOUIS ARMSTRONG · SOCRATES · LUCIANO PAVAROTTI

John T. Capps III, president of Bald Headed Men of America

"'Not the real you'? Well, of course it's not the real you. The real you is bald."

Boulder, Colorado, is considering a similar ploy.

While Morehead City, North Carolina, might appear to be the dark horse entry in such a heady field, it should not be counted out. As the international headquarters of BHMA (Bald Headed Men of America), and the hometown of its founder and president, John T. Capps III, Morehead City certainly gets the votes and backing of the 33,000 members the organization boasts through every state in the U.S.A., and in 13 other countries.

Should such an edifice come to be—and why should it not be called the Pleasure Dome?—*The Balder the Better* humbly nominates the following ten people as charter members worthy of that honor beyond all doubt.

1. Patrick Stewart—aka, Captain Jean-Luc Picard of "Star Trek: The Next Generation." For baldly going where no man has gone before. For showing all of those superior civilizations from distant galaxies that we are just as clever, and just as bald, and just as evolved as they are. When Ralph Kramden on "The Honeymooners" coined the expression "... to the moon, Alice," who ever dreamed it would lead to this?

2. John T. Capps III, of Bald Drive, Morehead City, North Carolina. Capps founded the Bald Headed Men of America back in 1972, and he tells his bald and balding brothers everywhere, "If you haven't got it, flaunt it!" A true believer in "outing," or exposing the phoniness of wigs, weaves, and transplants, he was recently asked to explain the difference between his group and the younger skinheads. "In a word," Capps replied, "attitude."

3. Michael Jordan demands big bucks for everything he looks at, smells, touches, wears, eats, thinks, or drinks. The only endorsement that doesn't slam dunk a quadrillion dollars into his bulging bank account is his selfless, ongoing promotion of baldness-as-lifestyle while playing basketball for the Chicago Bulls.

4. Sinéad O'Connor, for her wonderful songs, and her Irish pluck, and the nerve to stick her head and her heart into other people's business whenever she smells hypocrisy.

Patrick Stewart ● *Michael Jordan*

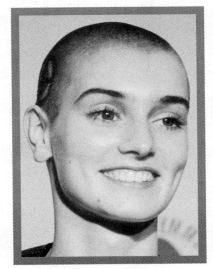 

Sinéad O'Connor ● *Donovan Bailey*

Stirling Moss ● *Doonesbury's Duke*

Daddy Warbucks ● *André Agassi*

5. Donovan Bailey, the Fastest Man in the World, for shaving his head and thereby critical moments off the previous Olympic and World records for the 100-meter sprint at the Atlanta Olympics in 1996. Given the fact that the energy required to produce hair is greater than that required to produce any other body tissue, the young Canadian doesn't waste any time getting rid of it.

6. Daddy Warbucks. What can we say that hasn't been said before? Capitalism and philanthropy came together close to sixty years ago, and LEAPIN' LIZARDS!, this man's shining dome has been a guiding light for little orphan girls ever since.

7. Sir Stirling Moss. A charter membership in the Bald Hall of Fame would be a perfect companion to the British racing driver's knighthood. On the track or off it, the man personifies dignity, coolness under pressure, and gentility.

MICHAEL STIPE • MALCOLM MUGGERIDGE • BOB HOSKINS • ISAAC HAYES

8. Hunter S. Thompson, the rebel with a thousand causes, for all of that fear and loathing, and for all of that sanity. Let's face it, if you open a Bald Hall of Fame and he's not in it, who's going to tell Mr. Duke?

9. Sean Connery, the Academy Award–winning Scottish actor, for getting better and better with each passing year. According to his legions of female fans around the world, at sixty-seven he is living, breathing, walking proof that Bald Is Beautiful, and sexy, and dreamy, and good, and . . .

10. André Agassi. Brooke Shields and Wimbledon aside, anything that might sound like the early rumblings of a bald supremacy movement has to be tied to this guy.

Sean Connery

Kiss This!

Did you know that in Albania the bald
head is worshiped erotically as
"the third buttock"?

Photography Credits

Page 2: AP Photo; *9*: AP Photo/Nick Ut; *27 (top)*: AP Photo; *27 (bottom)*: Canapress/Fisher; *31*: Wide World Photo; *40 (top)*: Canapress; *40 (middle)*: Canapress/A. Villiers; *40 (bottom)*: Wide World Photo; *42 (top)*: APN News Features; *42 (middle)*: AP Photo; *42 (bottom)*: AP Photo; *44 (top)*: Sigrid Estrada; *44 (middle)*: Denise Grant; *44 (bottom)*: AP News Library; *45*: AP Photo; *46*: AP Photo; *54 (top)*: Reuters; *54 (bottom)*: AP Photo/HO/Capital Cities/ABC; *56 (top)*: AP Photo; *56 (middle)*: Canapress; *56 (bottom)*: AP Photo/Bruno Mosconi; *60 (top)*: AP Photo; *60 (bottom)*: Canapress; *61 (top left)*: AP Photo; *61 (top right)*: Canapress; *61 (bottom)*: AP Photo/Jacques Brinon; *74*: AP Photo; *76 (top)*: Reuters; *76 (bottom)*: AP Photo; *78 (top)*: AP Photo/Tim Johnson; *78 (bottom)*: AP Photo/Chris Pizzello; *79 (top)*: AP Photo/Paul Sakuma; *79 (bottom)*: AP Photo; *86*: Toronto Star; *88 (top)*: AP Photo/Chris Martinez; *88 (bottom)*: AP Photo/Ron Frehm; *89 (top)*: AP Photo/Duane Burleson; *89 (bottom)*: AP Photo/Bill Sikes; *90 (top)*: Montreal Gazette/Dave Sidaway; *90 (bottom)*: CP Photo; *91 (top)*: Reuters/Mike Segar/Archive Photos; *91 (bottom)*: Wide World Photo; *94*: John T. Capps III; *98 (top left)*: Paramount Pictures; *98 (top right)*: Reuters; *98 (bottom left)*: Wide World Photo; *98 (bottom right)*: Toronto Star; *99 (top left)*: AP Photo; *99 (top right)*: Universal Press Syndicate; *99 (bottom left)*: Tribune Media Services; *99 (bottom right)*: AP Photo/Melbourne Age; *102*: AP Photo.

BURL IVES · DWIGHT D. EISENHOWER · JULIUS CAESAR · ZERO MOSTEL